The UNITED STATES PRESIDENTS

★ ★ Warren G. ★ ★

HARDING

Heidi M.D. Elston

Big Buddy Books
An Imprint of Abdo Publishing
abdopublishing.com

abdopublishing.com

Published by Abdo Publishing, a division of ABDO, PO Box 398166, Minneapolis, Minnesota 55439.
Copyright © 2017 by Abdo Consulting Group, Inc. International copyrights reserved in all countries. No
part of this book may be reproduced in any form without written permission from the publisher. Big Buddy
Books™ is a trademark and logo of Abdo Publishing.

Printed in the United States of America, North Mankato, Minnesota
062016
092016

Design: Sarah DeYoung, Mighty Media, Inc.
Production: Mighty Media, Inc.
Editor: Lauren Kukla
Cover Photograph: Corbis
Interior Photographs: AP Images (p. 19); Corbis (pp. 5, 6, 7, 9, 11); Getty Images (pp. 23, 27, 29);
    Ohio Historical Society (pp. 7, 13, 15, 21); Picture History (pp. 17, 25)

Cataloging-in-Publication Data

Names: Elston, Heidi M.D., author.
Title: Warren G. Harding / by Heidi M.D. Elston.
Description: Minneapolis, MN : Abdo Publishing, [2017] | Series: United States
    presidents | Includes bibliographical references and index.
Identifiers: LCCN 2015957541 | ISBN 9781680780963 (lib. bdg.) |
    ISBN 9781680775167 (ebook)
Subjects: LCSH: Harding, Warren G. (Warren Gamaliel), 1865-1923--Juvenile
    literature. | Presidents--United States--Biography--Juvenile literature. |
    United States--Politics and government--1921-1923--Juvenile literature.
Classification: DDC 973.91/4092 [B]--dc23
LC record available at http://lccn.loc.gov/2015957541

Contents

Warren G. Harding

Warren G. Harding was the twenty-ninth president of the United States. He was elected in 1920. At the time, many Americans were out of work and had little money. Harding promised to return the country to a simpler, easier time.

Harding was an honest president who worked hard for Americans. After less than three years in office, Harding died. However, his ideas impacted the **politics** of the **Republican** Party through the 1920s.

Timeline

1865
On November 2,
Warren Gamaliel Harding
was born in Corsica, Ohio.

1914
Harding won
election to the
US Senate.

1898
Harding won
election to the
Ohio state senate.

1918
The **Allies** won World War I.

1917
The United States entered **World War I**.

1920
On November 2, Harding was elected president of the United States.

1923
On August 2, President Warren G. Harding died.

7

Ohio Childhood

Warren Gamaliel Harding was born on November 2, 1865, in Corsica, Ohio. His parents were George and Phoebe Harding. Warren went to a one-room school. When he was 14, he entered Ohio Central College in Iberia, Ohio.

★ **FAST FACTS** ★

Born: November 2, 1865

Wife: Florence Kling DeWolfe (1860–1924)

Children: none

Political Party: Republican

Age at Inauguration: 55

Years Served: 1921–1923

Vice President: Calvin Coolidge

Died: August 2, 1923, age 57

George Harding (*left*) farmed. He was also a country doctor and a trader. Phoebe (*right*) helped women with childbirth.

First Jobs

After finishing college in 1882, Harding moved to Marion, Ohio. During this time, he held many jobs. He taught school. He also studied law. Then, he tried selling **insurance**.

At age 19, Harding became a reporter for the *Mirror*. This was a **Democratic** newspaper. However, Harding was a **Republican**.

In 1884, there was a presidential election. Harding **supported** Republican James G. Blaine in the election. This upset the newspaper owners. So, they fired Harding.

Harding later said teaching was "the hardest job I ever had."

The *Marion Star*

A few weeks after being fired, Harding moved to a different paper. The *Marion Star* was for sale. He and two friends bought the paper.

Harding worked day and night. He wanted the newspaper to succeed. He got help after he married Florence Kling DeWolfe in 1891.

Mrs. Harding soon began working at the *Marion Star*. Harding trusted his wife's good business sense. She took over running the newspaper. Mrs. Harding's hard work made it a success.

Harding working
at the *Marion Star*

Entering Politics

With his wife running the paper, Harding had time for other interests. He decided to enter **politics**. Harding was elected to the Ohio state senate in 1898. He was reelected in 1901.

Harding ran for governor of Ohio in 1910. But he lost the election. Harding's time in politics seemed to be over.

Then in 1912, Harding gave a speech. In it, he announced President William Taft's **nomination** for reelection. Harding's speech **impressed** leaders in the **Republican** Party.

The Hardings built this home in Marion, Ohio, in 1891. Harding worked on his 1920 presidential campaign from the home's large porch.

Senator Harding

In 1914, Harding ran for the US Senate. He easily won the election. During this time, many countries were fighting **World War I**. President Woodrow Wilson wanted the United States to enter the war. He hoped to help the **Allies** win.

Most senators, including Harding, agreed with Wilson. So, the United States joined the war in 1917. In November 1918, the Allies won. On June 28, 1919, a **treaty** was signed in France. This officially created peace between Germany and the Allies.

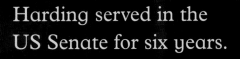

Harding served in the
US Senate for six years.

Prohibition

As senator, Harding voted for the Eighteenth **Amendment** to the **Constitution**. This made it illegal to make and sell **alcohol**. This was also known as the Prohibition Amendment.

The amendment passed in 1919. It ended the legal sale of alcohol in America. But people did not stop drinking it. A new kind of **criminal** appeared. Bootleggers illegally sold alcohol.

★ DID YOU KNOW? ★

Harding was the first president to give a speech over the radio.

Al Capone is one of the most famous bootleggers in US history. He made about $60 million a year selling alcohol.

Voting Women

In 1919, Senator Harding also voted for the Nineteenth **Amendment**. It would give women in all states the right to vote. Wyoming's **constitution** already allowed women to vote. It was the first state to give this right to women.

Other states followed. By 1918, 15 states gave women equal voting rights. People continued fighting for equal voting rights for women throughout the country. The Nineteenth Amendment finally became part of the US Constitution on August 26, 1920.

Because of the Nineteenth Amendment, Mrs. Harding was able to vote for her husband.

The 1920 Election

In 1920, Harding wanted to run for senator again. But later that year, the **Republicans** chose him to run for president. Harding ran against **Democrat** James M. Cox.

At this time, the US **economy** was suffering. Businesses were failing, and people were losing their jobs. Americans blamed President Wilson and his fellow Democrats.

Harding promised to make the country better. His **slogan** was "Back to **Normalcy**." On November 2, Harding won the election!

Calvin Coolidge (*left*) ran as Harding's vice president.

President Harding

On March 4, 1921, Harding became the twenty-ninth US president. He wanted to improve the **economy**. To accomplish this, President Harding **supported** several new laws.

Harding allowed US businesses to produce more goods. He also lowered taxes on goods made in America. But then he raised taxes on goods from other countries.

Harding also helped workers. Many large steel companies had 12-hour workdays. Harding got the companies to shorten their workdays.

PRESIDENT HARDING'S CABINET

March 4, 1921–August 2, 1923

★ **STATE:** Charles Evans Hughes
★ **TREASURY:** Andrew W. Mellon
★ **WAR:** John Wingate Weeks
★ **NAVY:** Edwin Denby
★ **ATTORNEY GENERAL:** Harry Micajah Daugherty
★ **INTERIOR:** Albert Bacon Fall,
Hubert Work (from March 5, 1923)
★ **AGRICULTURE:** Henry Cantwell Wallace
★ **COMMERCE:** Herbert Hoover
★ **LABOR:** James John Davis

President Harding (*seated, third from right*), Vice President Calvin Coolidge (*seated, second from right*), and cabinet members

Scandal

The American people trusted Harding. But, a **scandal** hurt his **administration**. Albert B. Fall was in Harding's **cabinet**. He was in charge of America's natural lands.

One such area was a piece of government land in Wyoming. Fall secretly allowed an oil company to drill on the land. The company gave Fall money in return.

SUPREME COURT ★ APPOINTMENTS

William Taft: 1921

George Sutherland: 1922

Pierce Butler: 1923

Edward T. Sanford: 1923

Albert B. Fall (*left*) went to jail for his part in the scandal.

Speaking Tour

Harding wanted to rebuild trust in his **administration**. So, in 1923, he began a speaking tour. He traveled across the country.

While in Seattle, Washington, Harding fell ill. He died in San Francisco, California, on August 2, 1923. Vice President Calvin Coolidge then became president.

Warren G. Harding was a popular president. Sadly, his presidency is remembered for the **scandals** in his **cabinet**. Still, Harding worked hard to be a good leader.

President and Mrs. Harding traveled together across the country on his speaking tour. Harding was the first president to visit Alaska and Canada while in office.

Office of the President

Branches of Government

The US government has three branches. They are the executive, legislative, and judicial branches. Each branch has some power over the others. This is called a system of checks and balances.

★ Executive Branch

The executive branch enforces laws. It is made up of the president, the vice president, and the president's cabinet. The president represents the United States around the world. He or she also signs bills into law and leads the military.

★ Legislative Branch

The legislative branch makes laws, maintains the military, and regulates trade. It also has the power to declare war. This branch includes the Senate and the House of Representatives. Together, these two houses form Congress.

★ Judicial Branch

The judicial branch interprets laws. It is made up of district courts, courts of appeals, and the Supreme Court. District courts try cases. Sometimes people disagree with a trial's outcome. Then he or she may appeal. If a court of appeals supports the ruling, a person may appeal to the Supreme Court.

Qualifications for Office

To be president, a candidate must be at least 35 years old. The person must be a natural-born US citizen. He or she must also have lived in the United States for at least 14 years.

Electoral College

The US presidential election is an indirect election. Voters from each state choose electors. These electors represent their state in the Electoral College. Each elector has one electoral vote. Electors cast their vote for the candidate with the highest number of votes from people in their state. A candidate must receive the majority of Electoral College votes to win.

Term of Office

Each president may be elected to two four-year terms. The presidential election is held on the Tuesday after the first Monday in November. The president is sworn in on January 20 of the following year. At that time, he or she takes the oath of office.
It states:

I do solemnly swear (or affirm) that I will faithfully execute the office of President of the United States, and will to the best of my ability, preserve, protect and defend the Constitution of the United States.

31

Line of Succession

The Presidential Succession Act of 1947 states who becomes president if the president cannot serve. The vice president is first in the line. Next are the Speaker of the House and the President Pro Tempore of the Senate. It may happen that none of these individuals is able to serve. Then the office falls to the president's cabinet members. They would take office in the order in which each department was created:

Secretary of State

Secretary of the Treasury

Secretary of Defense

Attorney General

Secretary of the Interior

Secretary of Agriculture

Secretary of Commerce

Secretary of Labor

Secretary of Health and Human Services

Secretary of Housing and Urban Development

Secretary of Transportation

Secretary of Energy

Secretary of Education

Secretary of Veterans Affairs

Secretary of Homeland Security

Benefits

★ While in office, the president receives a salary. It is $400,000 per year. He or she lives in the White House. The president also has 24-hour Secret Service protection.

★ The president may travel on a Boeing 747 jet. This special jet is called Air Force One. It can hold 70 passengers. It has kitchens, a dining room, sleeping areas, and more. Air Force One can fly halfway around the world before needing to refuel. It can even refuel in flight!

★ When the president travels by car, he or she uses Cadillac One. It is a Cadillac Deville that has been modified. The car has heavy armor and communications systems. The president may even take Cadillac One along when visiting other countries.

★ The president also travels on a helicopter. It is called Marine One. It may also be taken along when the president visits other countries.

★ Sometimes the president needs to get away with family and friends. Camp David is the official presidential retreat. It is located in Maryland. The US Navy maintains the retreat. The US Marine Corps keeps it secure. The camp offers swimming, tennis, golf, and hiking.

★ When the president leaves office, he or she receives lifetime Secret Service protection. He or she also receives a yearly pension of $203,700. The former president also receives money for office space, supplies, and staff.

PRESIDENTS AND THEIR TERMS

PRESIDENT	PARTY	TOOK OFFICE	LEFT OFFICE	TERMS SERVED	VICE PRESIDENT
George Washington	None	April 30, 1789	March 4, 1797	Two	John Adams
John Adams	Federalist	March 4, 1797	March 4, 1801	One	Thomas Jefferson
Thomas Jefferson	Democratic-Republican	March 4, 1801	March 4, 1809	Two	Aaron Burr, George Clinton
James Madison	Democratic-Republican	March 4, 1809	March 4, 1817	Two	George Clinton, Elbridge Gerry
James Monroe	Democratic-Republican	March 4, 1817	March 4, 1825	Two	Daniel D. Tompkins
John Quincy Adams	Democratic-Republican	March 4, 1825	March 4, 1829	One	John C. Calhoun
Andrew Jackson	Democrat	March 4, 1829	March 4, 1837	Two	John C. Calhoun, Martin Van Buren
Martin Van Buren	Democrat	March 4, 1837	March 4, 1841	One	Richard M. Johnson
William H. Harrison	Whig	March 4, 1841	April 4, 1841	Died During First Term	John Tyler
John Tyler	Whig	April 6, 1841	March 4, 1845	Completed Harrison's Term	Office Vacant
James K. Polk	Democrat	March 4, 1845	March 4, 1849	One	George M. Dallas
Zachary Taylor	Whig	March 5, 1849	July 9, 1850	Died During First Term	Millard Fillmore

PRESIDENT	PARTY	TOOK OFFICE	LEFT OFFICE	TERMS SERVED	VICE PRESIDENT
Millard Fillmore	Whig	July 10, 1850	March 4, 1853	Completed Taylor's Term	Office Vacant
Franklin Pierce	Democrat	March 4, 1853	March 4, 1857	One	William R.D. King
James Buchanan	Democrat	March 4, 1857	March 4, 1861	One	John C. Breckinridge
Abraham Lincoln	Republican	March 4, 1861	April 15, 1865	Served One Term, Died During Second Term	Hannibal Hamlin, Andrew Johnson
Andrew Johnson	Democrat	April 15, 1865	March 4, 1869	Completed Lincoln's Second Term	Office Vacant
Ulysses S. Grant	Republican	March 4, 1869	March 4, 1877	Two	Schuyler Colfax, Henry Wilson
Rutherford B. Hayes	Republican	March 3, 1877	March 4, 1881	One	William A. Wheeler
James A. Garfield	Republican	March 4, 1881	September 19, 1881	Died During First Term	Chester Arthur
Chester Arthur	Republican	September 20, 1881	March 4, 1885	Completed Garfield's Term	Office Vacant
Grover Cleveland	Democrat	March 4, 1885	March 4, 1889	One	Thomas A. Hendricks
Benjamin Harrison	Republican	March 4, 1889	March 4, 1893	One	Levi P. Morton
Grover Cleveland	Democrat	March 4, 1893	March 4, 1897	One	Adlai E. Stevenson
William McKinley	Republican	March 4, 1897	September 14, 1901	Served One Term, Died During Second Term	Garret A. Hobart, Theodore Roosevelt

PRESIDENT	PARTY	TOOK OFFICE	LEFT OFFICE	TERMS SERVED	VICE PRESIDENT
Theodore Roosevelt	Republican	September 14, 1901	March 4, 1909	Completed McKinley's Second Term, Served One Term	Office Vacant, Charles Fairbanks
William Taft	Republican	March 4, 1909	March 4, 1913	One	James S. Sherman
Woodrow Wilson	Democrat	March 4, 1913	March 4, 1921	Two	Thomas R. Marshall
Warren G. Harding	Republican	March 4, 1921	August 2, 1923	Died During First Term	Calvin Coolidge
Calvin Coolidge	Republican	August 3, 1923	March 4, 1929	Completed Harding's Term, Served One Term	Office Vacant, Charles Dawes
Herbert Hoover	Republican	March 4, 1929	March 4, 1933	One	Charles Curtis
Franklin D. Roosevelt	Democrat	March 4, 1933	April 12, 1945	Served Three Terms, Died During Fourth Term	John Nance Garner, Henry A. Wallace, Harry S. Truman
Harry S. Truman	Democrat	April 12, 1945	January 20, 1953	Completed Roosevelt's Fourth Term, Served One Term	Office Vacant, Alben Barkley
Dwight D. Eisenhower	Republican	January 20, 1953	January 20, 1961	Two	Richard Nixon
John F. Kennedy	Democrat	January 20, 1961	November 22, 1963	Died During First Term	Lyndon B. Johnson
Lyndon B. Johnson	Democrat	November 22, 1963	January 20, 1969	Completed Kennedy's Term, Served One Term	Office Vacant, Hubert H. Humphrey
Richard Nixon	Republican	January 20, 1969	August 9, 1974	Completed First Term, Resigned During Second Term	Spiro T. Agnew, Gerald Ford

PRESIDENT	PARTY	TOOK OFFICE	LEFT OFFICE	TERMS SERVED	VICE PRESIDENT
Gerald Ford	Republican	August 9, 1974	January 20, 1977	Completed Nixon's Second Term	Nelson A. Rockefeller
Jimmy Carter	Democrat	January 20, 1977	January 20, 1981	One	Walter Mondale
Ronald Reagan	Republican	January 20, 1981	January 20, 1989	Two	George H.W. Bush
George H.W. Bush	Republican	January 20, 1989	January 20, 1993	One	Dan Quayle
Bill Clinton	Democrat	January 20, 1993	January 20, 2001	Two	Al Gore
George W. Bush	Republican	January 20, 2001	January 20, 2009	Two	Dick Cheney
Barack Obama	Democrat	January 20, 2009	January 20, 2017	Two	Joe Biden

"We must have a citizenship less concerned about what the government can do for it and more anxious about what it can do for the nation." Warren G. Harding

★ WRITE TO THE PRESIDENT ★

You may write to the president at:
The White House
1600 Pennsylvania Avenue NW
Washington, DC 20500

You may e-mail the president at:
comments@whitehouse.gov

37

Glossary

administration (uhd-mih-nuh-STRAY-shuhn)—a group of people that manages an operation, a department, or an office.

alcohol—an adult beverage, such as beer, wine, or whiskey.

allies—people, groups, or nations working together. During World War I, Great Britain, France, Russia, Italy, and Japan were called the Allies.

amendment—a change to a country's or a state's constitution.

cabinet—a group of advisers chosen by the president to lead government departments.

constitution (kahnt-stuh-TOO-shuhn)—the basic laws that govern a country or a state.

criminal (KRIH-muh-nuhl)—someone who has broken the law.

Democrat—a member of the Democratic political party.

economy—the way that a country produces, sells, and buys goods and services.

impress—to cause someone to feel admiration or respect.

insurance—a contract that promises to guard people against a loss of money if something happens to them or their property.

nomination—the state of being named as a possible winner.

normal—typical or usual. The state of being normal is normalcy.

politics—the art or science of government. Something referring to politics is political. A person who is active in politics is a politician.

Republican—a member of the Republican political party.

scandal—an action that shocks people and disgraces those connected with it.

slogan—a word or a phrase used to express a position, a stand, or a goal.

support—to believe in or be in favor of something.

treaty—an agreement made between two or more groups.

World War I—a war fought in Europe from 1914 to 1918.

★ WEBSITES ★

To learn more about the US Presidents, visit **booklinks.abdopublishing.com**. These links are routinely monitored and updated to provide the most current information available.

Index